CW01163282

This Firm Foundation – Contemporary Bath Abbey Life

An epic poem

By

Meryl M Williams

The Poet Meryl M Williams b1966

Meryl was born in South Wales and studied bio-medical sciences in Cardiff before working in the field of Medical Research in London, Bath and Texas, USA. She returned to Bath to write poetry, then prose and this is her first epic poem.

©M Williams, 2025

ISBN: 9781917601795

hB

Other works by the same Poet and Author.

Poetry with Photographs

Moods in Bloom
A Waterfall of Words

Autobiography

Treasure Within – A Memoir

Novellas

The Judge Jones Trilogy
Judge Jones Resurgam

My Lady's Sovereign
Mortymer House

CONTENTS LIST

This Firm Foundation.	Page no.
Part One – Abbey Folk.	4
Part Two – Milk and Honey.	33
Part Three – Music and Song.	55
Part Four – Come Inside!	62
Index of Images.	71
References.	72

Locus iste, a Deo factus est...

> This place was made by God.

Part One – Abbey Folk

I had no notion, in the past,
That bells are rung within, without
A peal of ten is clapper sounded
But the Carillon plays a hymn
With hammers outside it.

> This latter moves my very soul
> With a touching sound so warm and real
> Computers can control this art
> While familiar hymns ring out apart.
>
> My guide for this amazing tour
> Describes a mathematical force
> A Coronation or Wedding peal
> Bells for a Grandsire, oh Tower speak!
>
> Tell, oh Tower, of ages gone
> Lives are living, sound the song
> Merry ringing, Easter Day
> Single toll to call us in

Wake all sleepers, worship here,
Then depart, to sin no more.

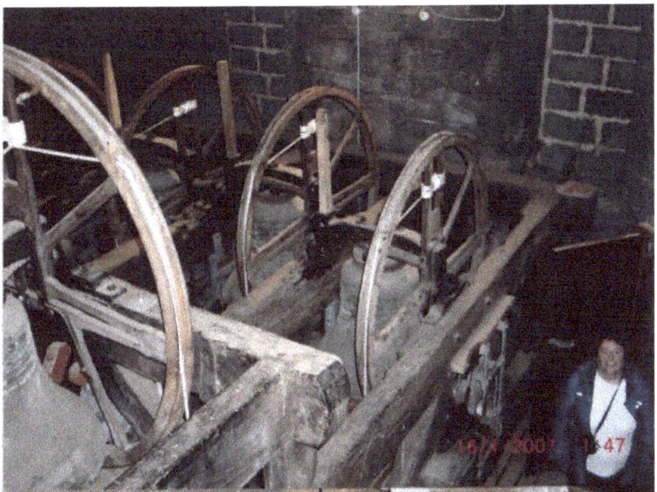
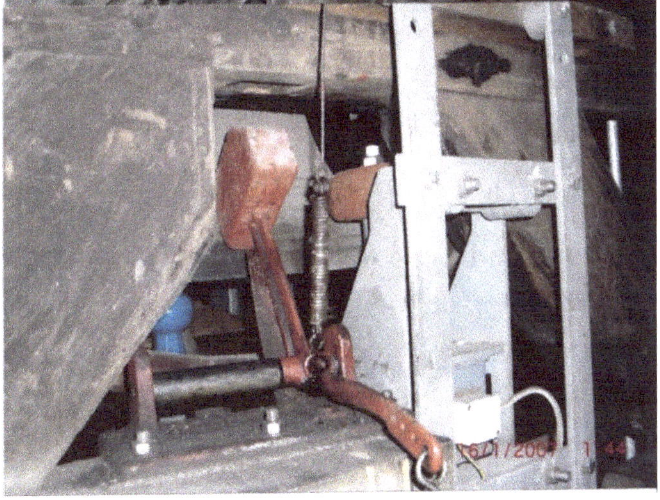

Easter dawned with chilly sun
I waited as I watched
A busker or a street musician
Was oblivious of the havoc they caused.
A colleague spoke, the bells rang on,
I found a volunteer.

A lovely lady at the door
Assessed, then went to tower floor
Those bells rang out like ne'er before
Rang out both loud and clear!
The peal continued on and on
At last I had my say
"The Bishop is to preach for us, it's glorious Easter Day".
I know how popular buskers are
With town and Corporation
But finally we had our say
That disrupting services had to stop
While our walls soundproofed must be,
I even emailed my MP!

The Rector of the day did find
That though he won the case in hand
The street musicians still play on

But when the big West doors are open,
Sunday sounds resound all around.

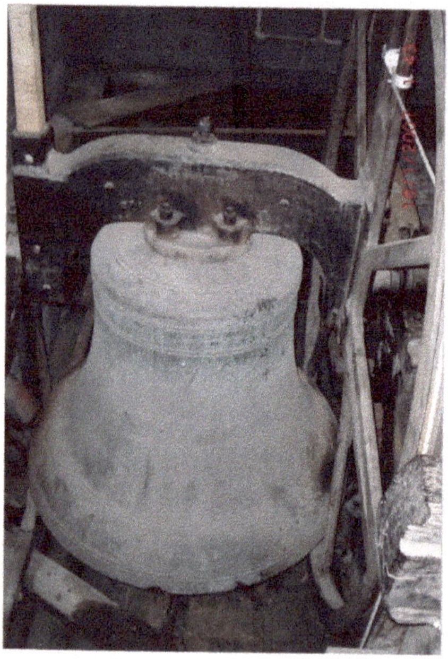

Ropes are seen in this next image
Taken where the ringers work
A hand Carillon plus looking back
You will see how levers pull
The bell rotates, the clapper sounds
Gravity makes a joyful noise.

Memory of a lovely group
Of hand bell ringers also came
From across the Pond, to play
At a daytime concert with superb display.

A popular Rector of his day
At our meeting, was heard to say
That people come from far and wide
To worship here at the Abbey, inside.

Parishioners are a small proportion
In theory as the Parish is just
A small piece of the City's whole
But many come from outside it's walls,
Folk from Bristol, Chippenham too
All unite to praise the Lord.

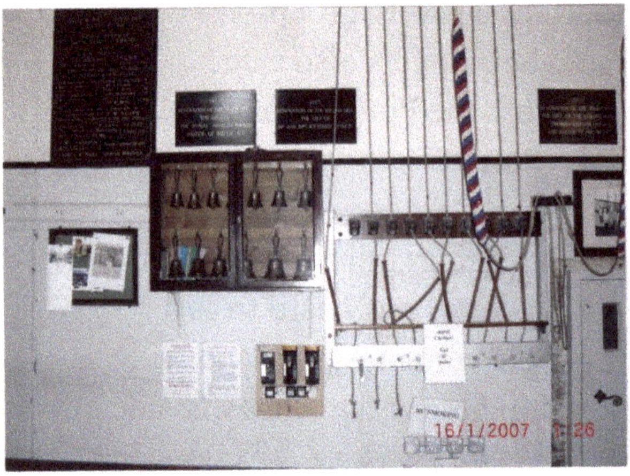
16/1/2007

See the view from top of Tower
In front, a dome of Pump Rooms roof
    Left you'll see our Roman Baths
    Away in front the Thermae Spa
    Baths to study, pools to bathe
    Captured in this digital age.

    Examine the second image
    The view from Tower Top
    You'll see the Spire of St. Michael without
    Once outside the City's walls
    Our sister church, whose Rector
    Once assisted the Abbey with worship
    Throughout an Interregnum
    As a new Rector for the Abbey, was
    sought.

    This was the case when I first came
    'Twas 1989 and the first thing I noticed
    On attending morning service,
    Was how one older clergyman
    Had military decoration on his blue and
    white robe.

    Another man dressed in red so I enquired
    of a friend

He serves Her Majesty the Queen,
A Royal Chaplain I was told.
Later after years had passed
I saw this once again
A Rector of Bath Abbey wore
Scarlet for his appointment
On television on Christmas Day
Broadcast to the Nation
With a big tree in a bright array.

Then as the nineties drew to a close
Before the turn of the Century
We teamed up with St Michael's church
For an Alpha Course finishing
With Holy Communion
At Freshford Bakery.

Many people joined this course
We made long lasting friends
And one of their number
Was a bell ringer for their church without
the walls!

After this enjoyment of spiritual
Nourishment, with a shared meal and talk
We drove to Devon for Lee Abbey

With its beautiful house and walks.

From the west front view all angels
Climbing ladder of Jacob's dream
Bishop Oliver's re- awakening
Built of stone from quarry hewn.

Here there is a gallery
On the outside of the wall
From here, on the rooftop,
The Bishop blesses all
Who may be gathered in the square
On the morn of glorious Easter Day.

Take a step away, a distance
View the windows from inside
Appreciate each detailed colour
Every pane a work of art.

Scenes all from the life of Jesus
A woman's perfume scents his feet
Tears are falling, washing, healing
Tresses wipe away her guilt
Apostles learn their Teacher's life.

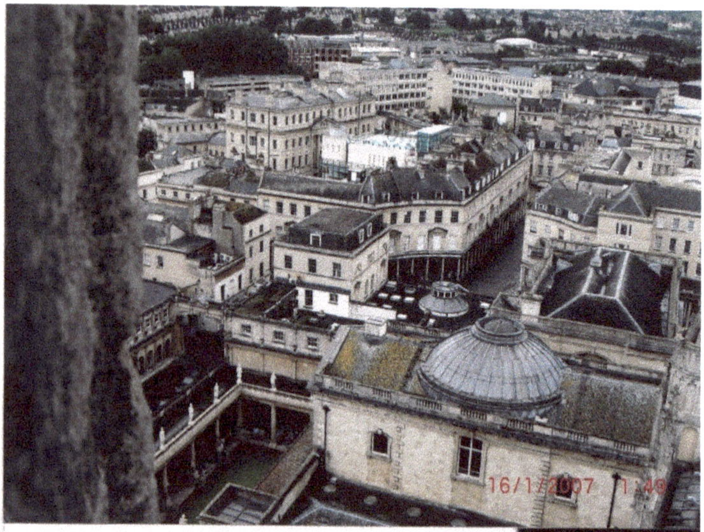

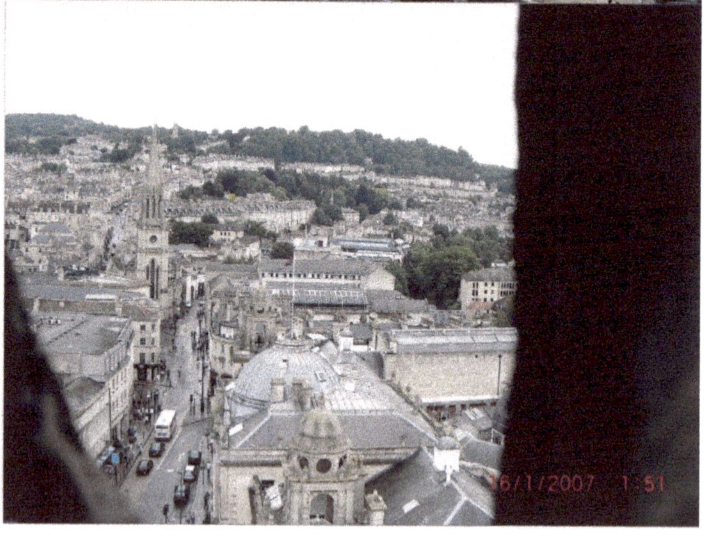

A Parish friend of long years standing
Lived throughout horrific War
Memory spoken for Remembrance
Cracking codes in days of yore.
Then she gently once confided
Stories of a health scare sort.
To the church I took her flowers
Then a tale of love we heard
      Sacrifice so hard to bear
      Tiny gains for freedom longing
      Precious lives lost overseas.

      Here's the lion with unicorn
      Atop our ancient Mineral
      A Hospital for many nations
      With its Chaplain, serves us too
      Opened three hundred years ago
      Now replaced, at last, anew.

      Caring Grandsire wooed and won
      Was a handsome Dorset boy
      Climbed the cliffs forever young
      His church so pretty, his life so long.
      Devotion to his inner calling
      Service, giving, raising funds
      Supporting younger generations

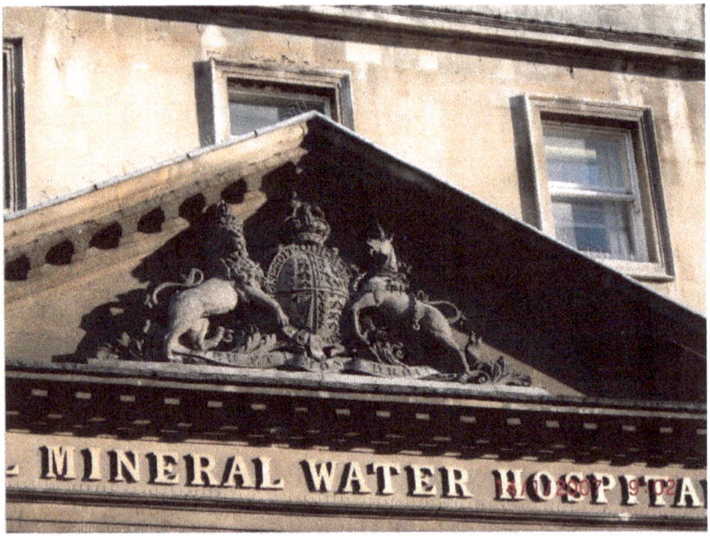
MINERAL WATER HOSPITA

I will honour memory fond.

 At our second, voluntary meeting
     How I valued expertise
     Yes this gadget can be posted
     Solar powered, no batteries.
     Memories of a local venue
     Where we shoeboxed all day long
     Power symbol of Christ's Passion
     Never forgotten, suspended cross
     One in Europe says our Rector
     Like the homegrown one at Wells
     Sister in our Diocese.

The solemn East end Sanctuary
Has fan vaulting as King's,
Cambridge you can see
But along the whole length of the Nave
It's a copy from Victorian Age.
There was an avenue of trees
A bowling alley uncovered too
Such a work the whole to restore
Shows the commitment of generations before.

    Grandsire moved into his best life

With the tender Abbey's young
Tiny child enjoying pastimes
While your keenest fan looked on.

Nearby across the city, at our sister local church
Fellowship was found with cousins
Traveling from across the Pond
A fine young man attended Abbey
We had tea in English style
Milk in first I must advise.

This young man drew inspiration
From a speech of Lincoln's own
Wore his college badge forever
Departed with our magazine,
Printed art work we had drawn.

Change of season brings new vicars
All for reasons of the best
When one retired, our Bishop joined us
Then to Canterbury he was led.

Yes we see so many faces
The small, the tall, the lovely talks
Different takes on Trinity Sunday

Rose windows, friendships, music chords.

Men and women everyday
Songsters, wardens, doctors, nurses
Lawyers, sweethearts, babes in arms
Baptisms for His Honour's daughters
Members of this family.

Then another and another, growing church spread out its wings
Fill the Nave that once was empty
Hope for every living thing.
Golden Age we threw a party
Five hundred years since Bishop's dream
Entertainment, food delivered by a kitchen from Glastonbury.

Then the city recognised, two thousand years
Of faith at this turn of the century
Millennial milestone marked by opening up
An ancient baths of warming springs
Celebrations running late, celebrities sing
Football arias while the Water keeps on flowing

Now the tourists keep on coming,
Handel's music played its part
I have a video, timeless joy preserved in my heart.

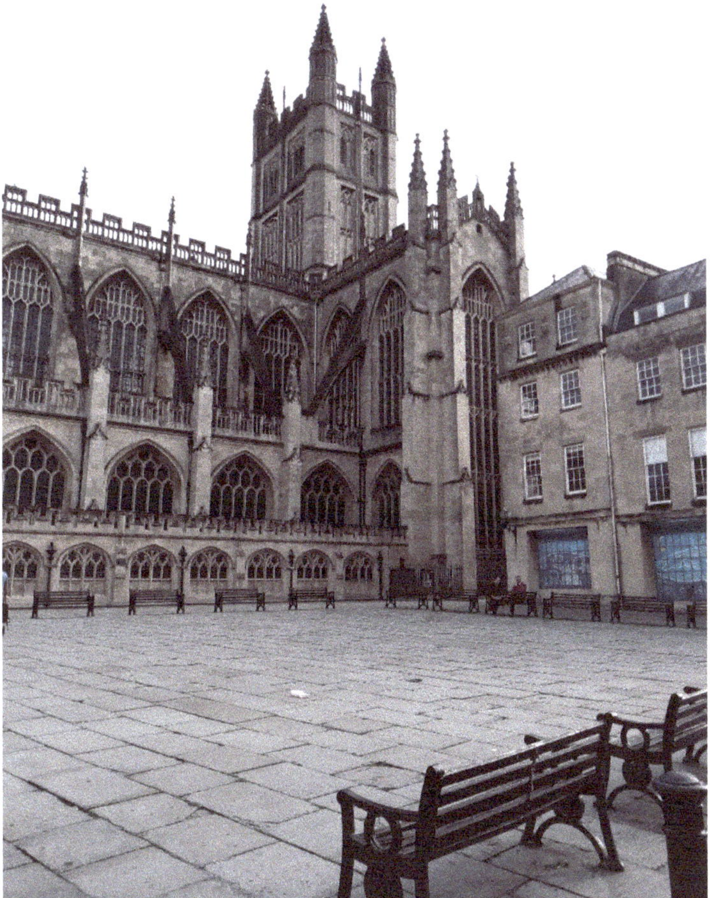

Then I dawdled in the Abbey
    Pausing to disturb your peace
    Where found you tulips in October?
    I had to know and thus she said
    A stall amazing by the wall
    Of our old friend the Mineral.
    'Twas true! 'Twas true! I bought them too!

    Then I crept in one weekday morn,
    To photograph an angel carved,
    For my website funding plan
    As my training for the walk began.

    Just a soupcon thus was raised
    But Footprint now is dream complete
    Safe our floor with hot springs heating
    Newly surfaced, stalls are back
    Lighting on the darkest night
    Lovely chandeliers kept, restored to
    former glories yet
    More is always called to action
    Song school started, hope ressurexit.

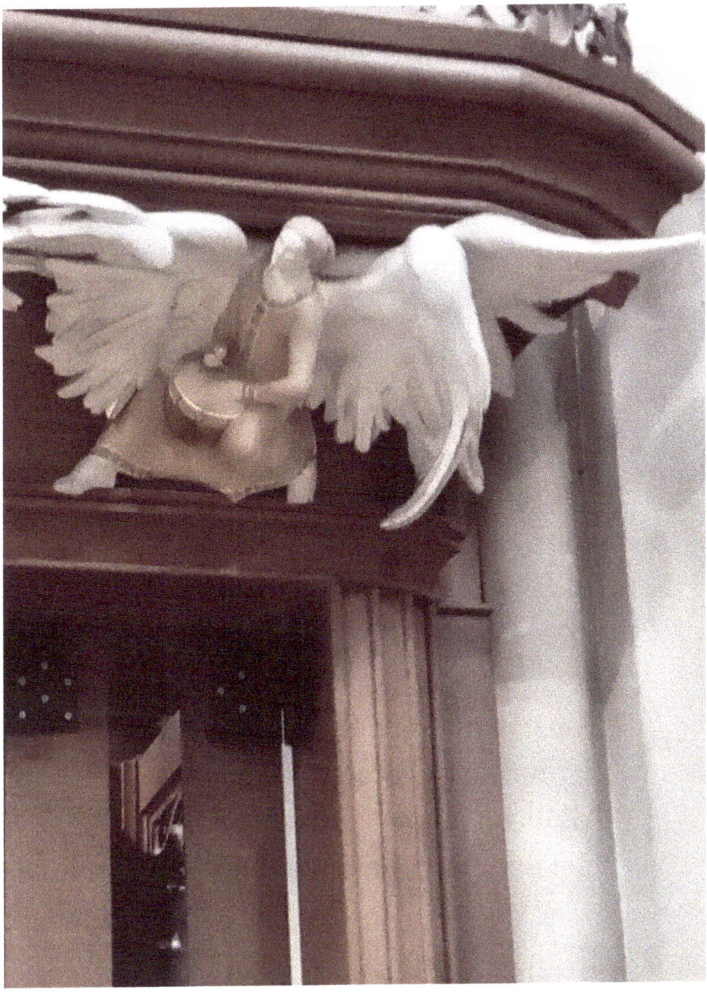

The Pinnacle atop the Abbey tower
    Dwarfs the door that leads to stairs
    Such strong perspective, visualised here
    Before the age of film or camera.

    Fan vaulting shows such sumptuous decoration
    But from the Victorian Age,
    While in the Eastern Sanctuary
    It's contemporaneous with Kings.

    One of the highlights of our Tower Tour
    Is a sight indeed quite rare
    You can spot from quite close by
    The inside cement of these fan effects
    From beneath the Abbey sky.

    You can also see the clock face
    In reverse as comes as a surprise
    All close up so worth the climb
    Just one hundred and eighty steps in time.

  The lovely lady mentioned before
Had also climbed up Salisbury's Tower

This is extra energetic, even more steps
 But only His Majesty is permitted on the spire.

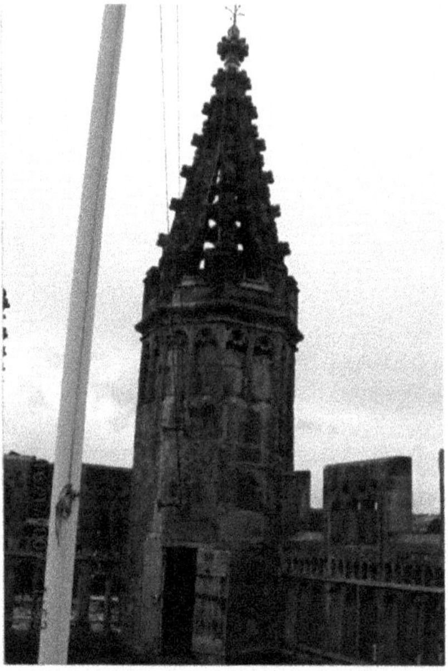

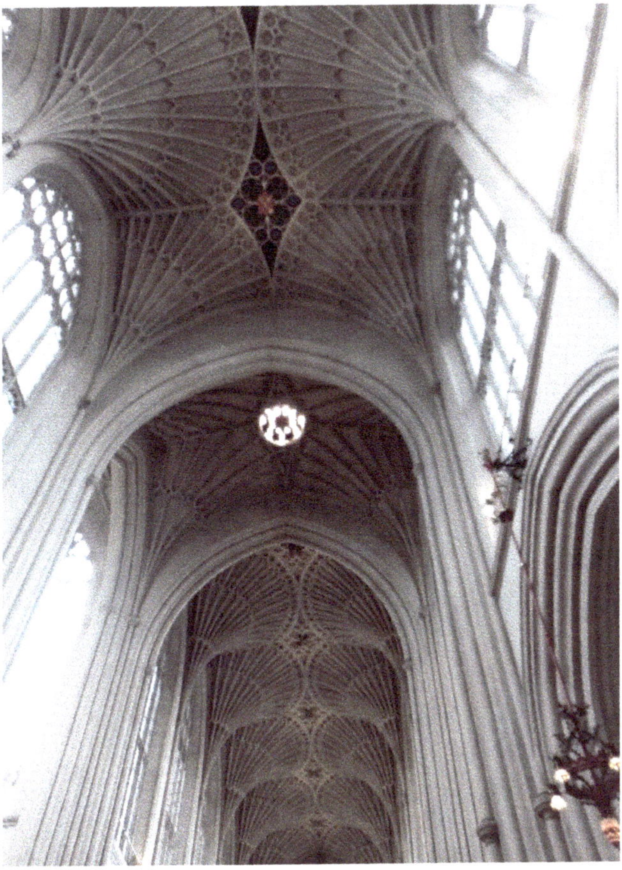

Next is the Chapel of Gethsemane
With candle always lit
For the prisoners of conscience
And book of Remembrance kept.

The pages of the book are turned
Such that names of the fallen
Should be revealed
For those who fought on foreign shores
Plus the lives lost in the Blitz at home.

The two chapels here are side by side
In the Birde chapel the sacrament resides
Both are open for private prayer
The small wooden font is found in here.

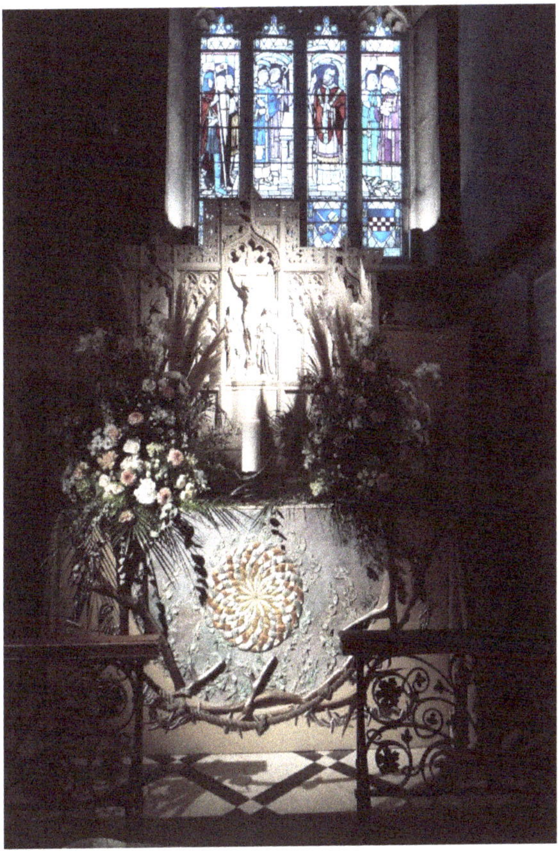

Come cries the Psalmist
Clash cymbals, strike the gong,
Make a joyful, merry noise
Unto this Heavenly throne.

From this Lectern hear the Word
Give thanks to God above
Raise your eyes up Heavenward
Share for ever in his love.

Exhibitions also take place
We've seen the moon, the earth displayed
A lovely artwork of butterflies
The superb calligraphy, with embroidery
That depicts the Gospels and the Old Testament
Showing familiar Bible stories here in this
Art form, so beautiful and so prized.

This wonderful depiction of the Nazarene
Demonstrates the fullness of the Prophecy
Brought to life in Jesus the Messiah
Shown in white with golden threads
From His birth until his glorious Ascension
All retold with incredible attention to detail.

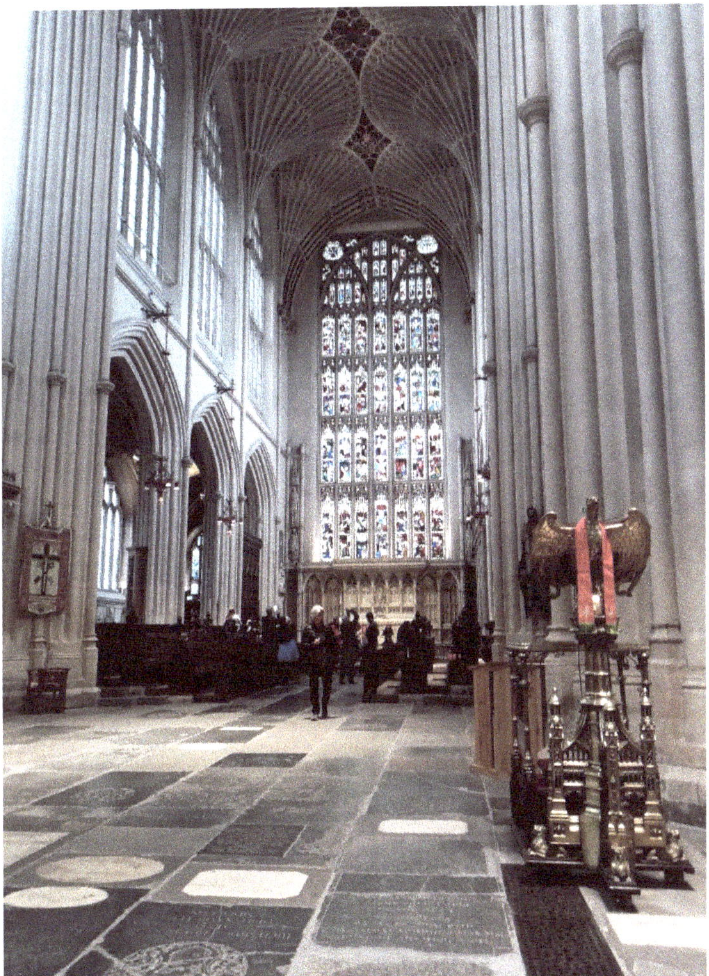

Part Two – Milk and Honey

Local Bath long held view dictates that
The sandstone of honeyed hue
Once was formed from tropical weather
With the sea reaching this far inland
Leaving rocks of weathered form
Soft for carving from early dawn.

Combe Down Mines can rightly claim
Work to quarry since Caesar's time
On a more industrial scale
When Ralph Allen rose to fame.

Romans, Saxons, Georgians too
Used this stone to make our view
Landscape chalky, waters hard
Sold as healthy, full of salts
Tastes 'delicious' says my relation
Bath's a time warp sings the bard.

At Bath Abbey find a guide
Learn so much of church inside
Here the window on North side
Shows coats of arms for distinguished dead
Gave their all to pay for the lead.

Next the view is shown below
From Camden Crescent, just half a bow
Tiny Abbey one mile away
Through the trees on a summer's day.

Perspective shows the Abbey leaning
While the pavement looks quite straight
Slight perhaps, exaggerated by my Tablet
This the East end showing me
A flying buttress like an ear.

This the view from Grand Parade
Above the Gardens of same name
It's said of some great churches so
The sanctuary comes first
To use for service at once
Then the remaining building works follow.

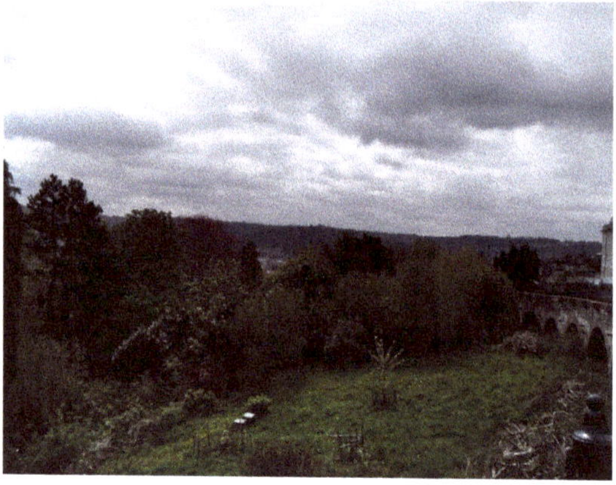

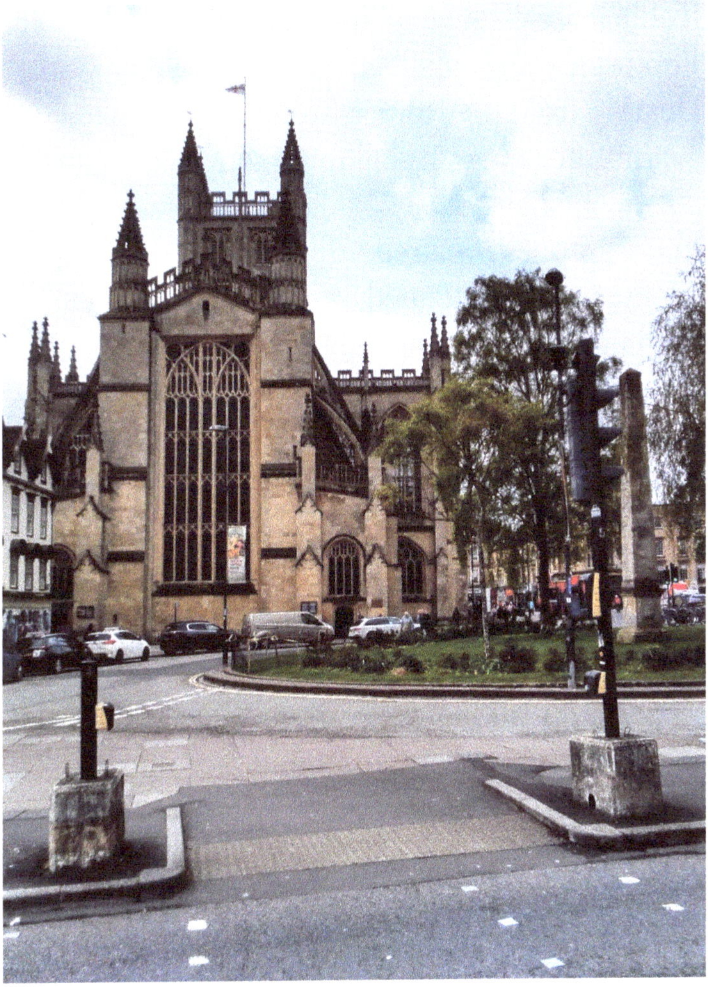

Rolling back the years once more
Footprint vision made safe our floor
Heating from the Roman springs
Warmth for every living thing.

Ledger stones repaired, made safe
Monuments catalogued, researched
Put neatly back in place,
New floor surface, all complete
Back our beautiful Corporation stalls
Carved and polished then the frontal
High Altar depicts a living waterfall.

Monday morning one fine day
A volunteer was heard to say
That during all the excavation
A cherub was unearthed, found face down
But beautifully preserved.

The carved young boy was sculptured sleeping
With an hourglass in his keeping
Holding on to branch of Cyprus
Near an urn of gorgeous detail.

Mystery at first surrounded
This quaint memorial, but research has shown

It's for a child called Catherine Malone.

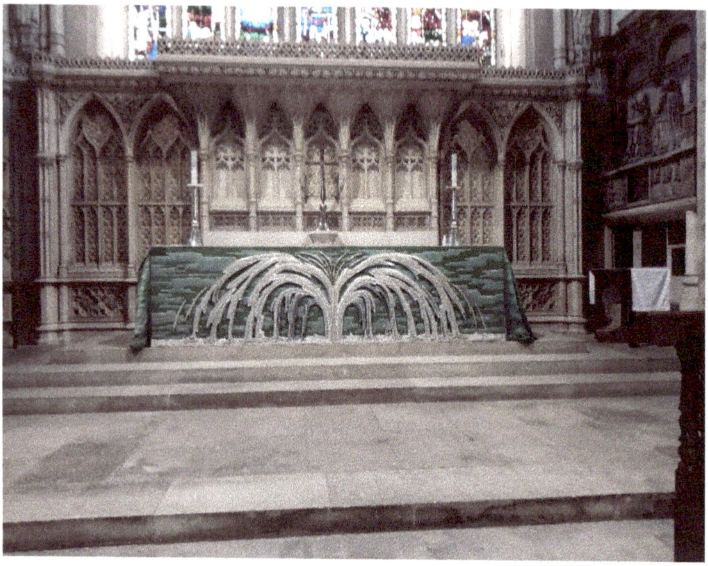

A group of ladies set to stitch
A frontal for a Nave Altar with praying hands
This was then inaugurated
Used for service and contemplated.

Part of Footprint's early dawn
When the planning stage was born
To have an altar as Lichfield Cathedral
On a dais that rises from the floor.

This next image does reveal
The steps inside of Lichfield's Nave
Their guide book shows an altered tale
Of how it's lowered, flush with floor.

One Rector was keen to have this same design
In Bath Abbey but what we've seen
Is that underneath we have no space
For all that hydraulic machinery
To raise the floor both up and down
As we did not dig deep or far
To preserve the building that we find.

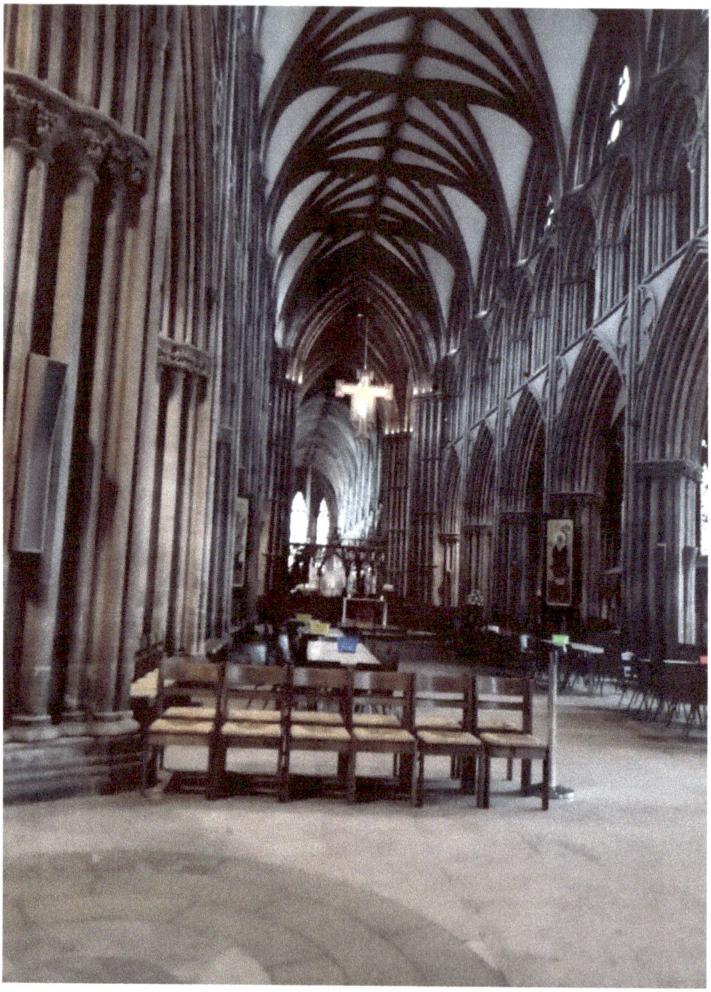

Here's an image of without
At Lichfield Cathedral, grand West Front
Two spires at either side shown here
A third at crossing, the only one like it
In the UK.

Take another long held look
At the icon from inside
Memory of St. John's Bathwick
Where the golden cross resides.

Hear the Rector of his day
Preach in Bath Abbey one November day
Of a church outside Berlin
Has an icon thus within.

Look again at Lichfield's inner
See an icon at the pillar
Finally an image next, sideways view
That demonstrates
Where the spires perfectly put
Show the crossing in symmetry.

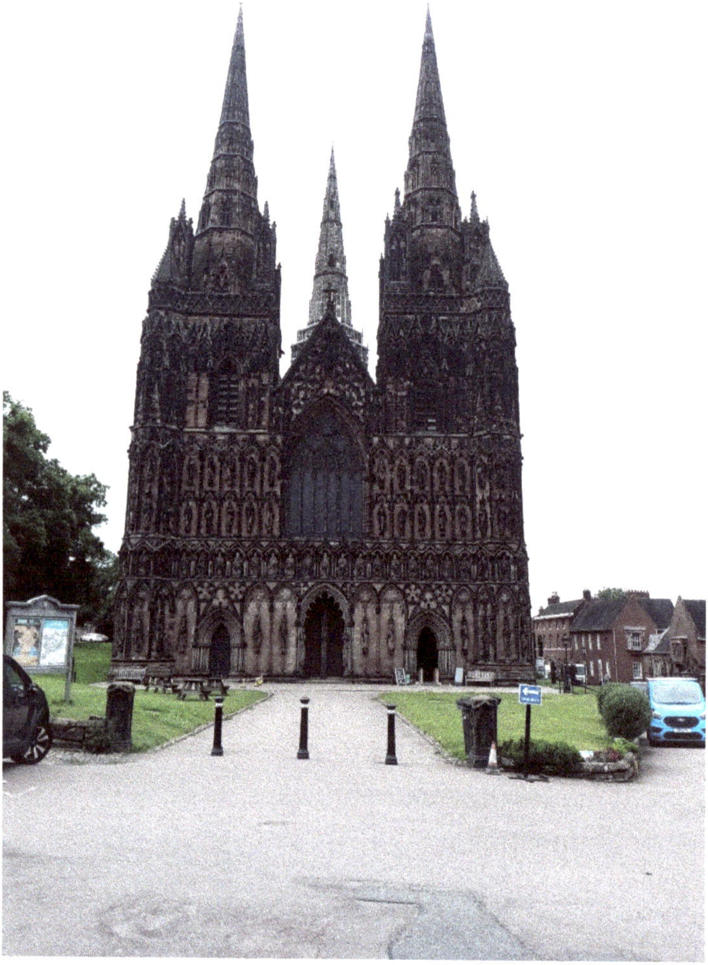

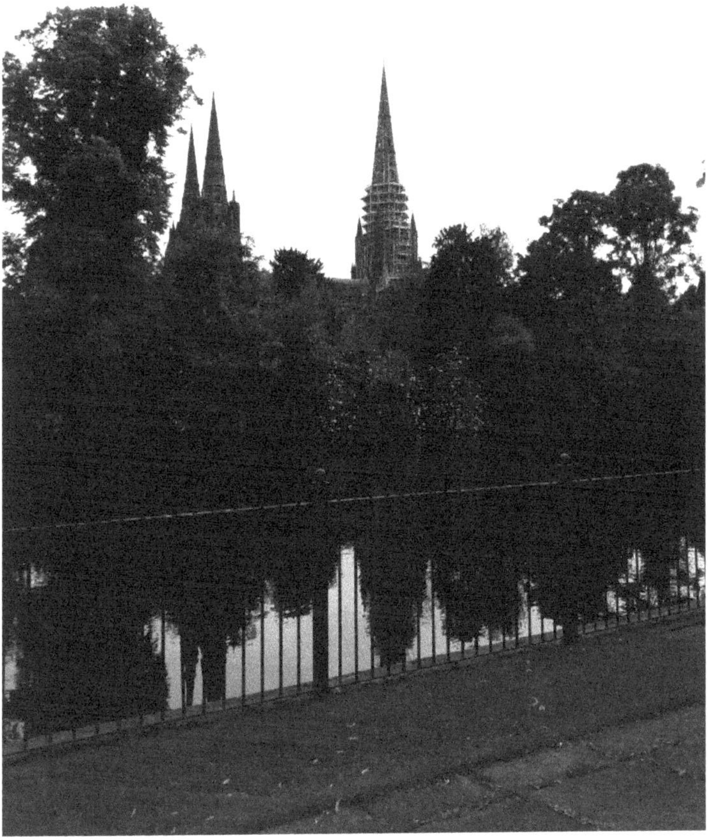

Back at Bath Abbey, as we've seen, the Chapel of Gethsemane
Has the prisoners of conscience candle lit
It will be found in South East Corner
With a vivid stained glass of perfume story.

See the woman, tresses falling
As she anoints our Lord's feet
Washing them with tears and calling
While forgiveness is complete.

This same famous Bible story
Is depicted once again
As a panel in the East Window
52 scenes from the life of Christ.

Pause to gaze at this vast window
You will see familiar images
One, the raising of Jairus' daughter
Repeated in an oil depiction
At our City's Victoria Art Gallery.

In another piece looking East
Lenten story shows Satan
Tempting Our Lord then crushed, departing
Entering the heart of Judas next.

Next I move to furthest corner
At the North side, staying East
Here you'll find St Alphege Chapel
With a frontal for the feast.
Wheat for harvest plus a lovely embroidery
Shows a scallop shell here replete.
In my quilt I used this motif
With ladies dancing, lords a leaping
This is for a memory.

Christmas Eve at Carol Praise
Sing with actions of the twelve days
Twirling, squatting, having fun
Every year it must be done.

This same pretty, little corner
By the door for Tower tours
The altar in St. Alphege Chapel
Has a lovely frontal shown below,

It's wheat symbolises our Journey through Faith
The Scallop Shell is for Pilgrimage
Beneath the Sarum Group stitchery
Is a stone originating at Canterbury.
Here we meet for Morning Prayer

Then, such delight, the organ starts.

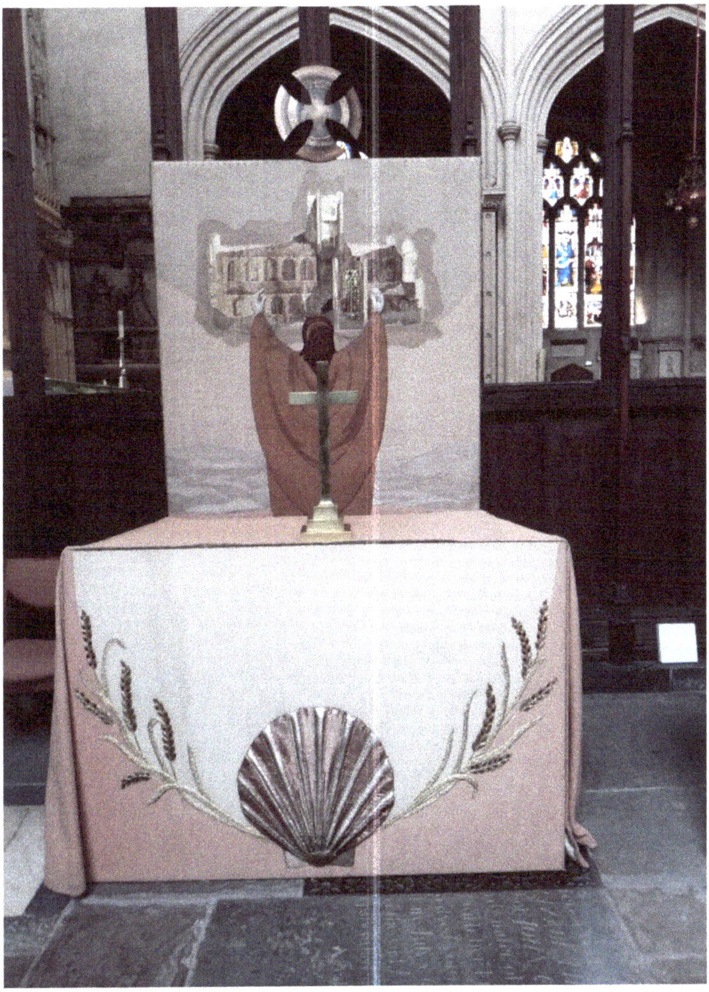

Now our attention turns to the right
This the South Transept with a spectacular tomb
A man, his wife in repose, wearing the costume
Of doublet and hose but his hairstyle suggesting
A resemblance to Shakespeare and the era of the
Sixteenth Century.
A very grand tomb, the figures in alabaster
Perhaps.

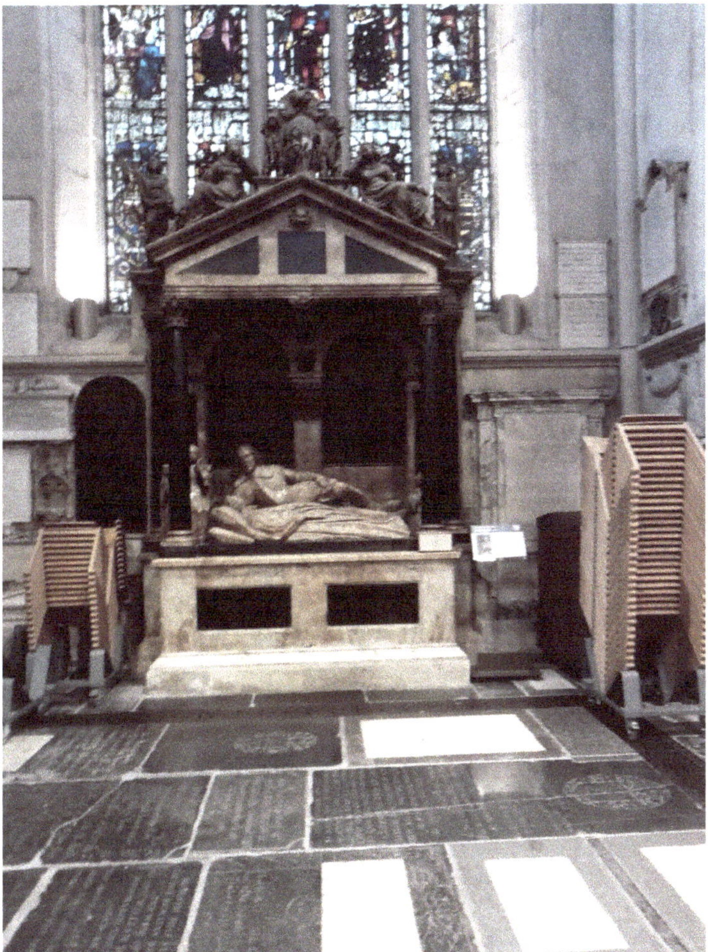

I have celebrated in words above
The turn of the Century with spa restored
Here's a statue of the risen Lord
Breaking bonds of death and Hell
Wounds of pain show compassionate love.

See to the right of this dear figure
A secret door that I suspect
Leads to the Vestry where staff robe up.

Above the door, such fond remembrance
A Narnia lamp post encapsulated in a modern
Social media post for a leader
Teaching, reading C.S. Lewis
Inspiring the young and all who listen.

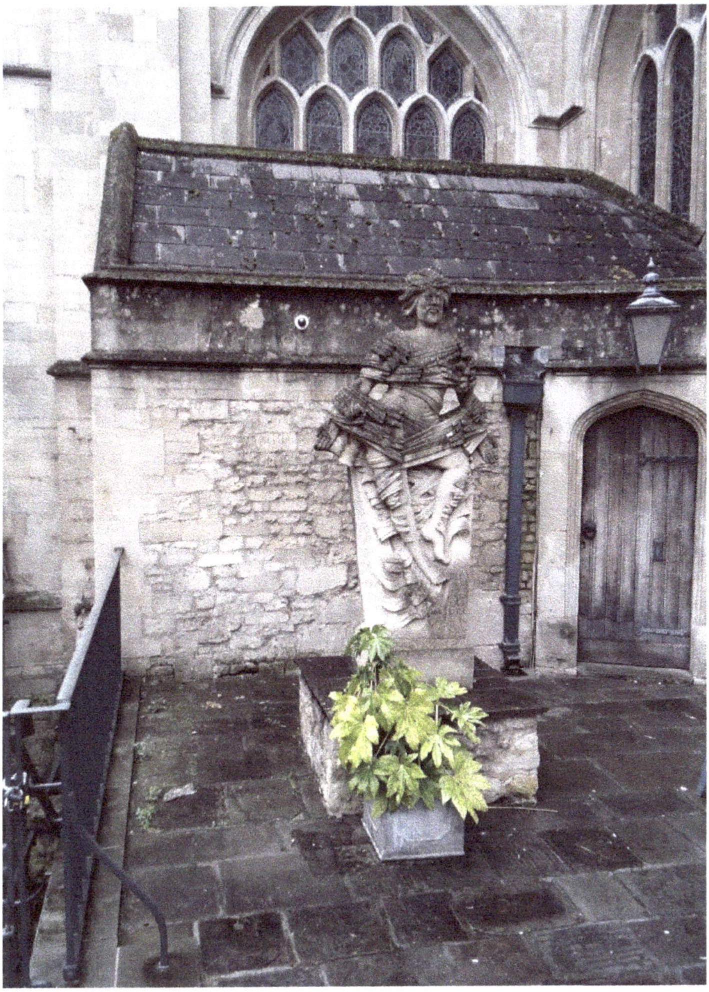

Our sister in the Diocese,
The home of Bishop's throne
The perfect, lovely Cathedra
That gives the church it's name.

See from the image, wonderment
An amazing scissor arch
It's from the fourteenth century
To support the Tower lest it leans
While all admirers can't help but exclaim
It really looks Contemporary!

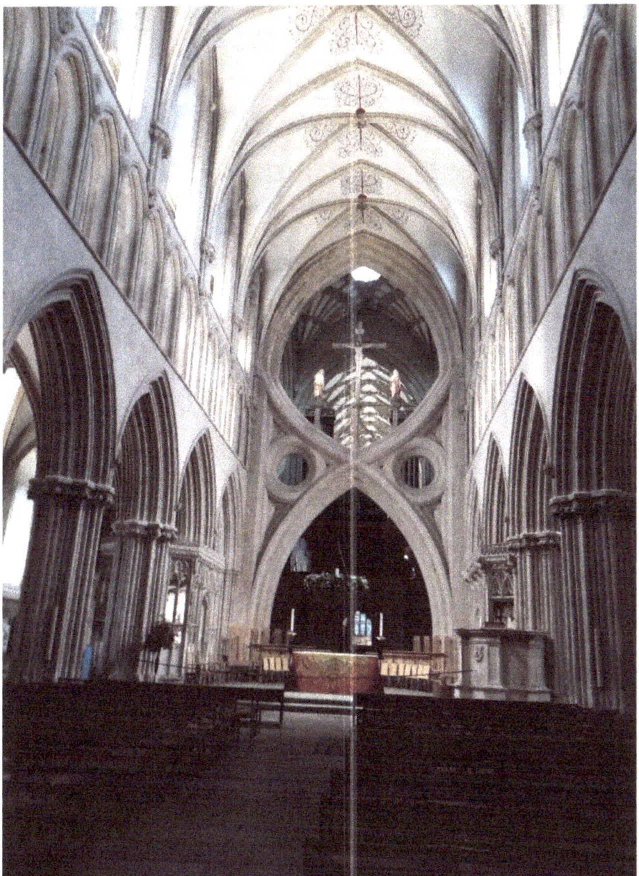

Part Three – Music and Song

Mighty Klais is fairly new
Built in the nineties, hear it tuned
Lovely just to feel the vibration
Knowing that they really care
Enough to make our worship perfectly shared.

Many happy hours are spent
Singing hymns or listening
Organ recitals on Easter Eve
All through summer, behind
Those beautiful carved angels
Where the choirs join in worship
Right throughout the church's year.

It all began with Advent Sunday
Watching, waiting, prayers and hope
Then the Christ child warmly welcomed
Celebrations for a King, adoration,
Joyous feasting, preparation before Lent comes in.

Melody Makers sang sublime, sweet music
A choir formed from local schools
Oh how proud their mums and dads

With a future now we have our own song school.

Rolling back to yesteryear
I came to Bath at the latter part of 20th Century
Parish Communion met in those carved
Victorian Corporation Stalls and dear sides men
Would show me to a seat.

They were so courteous and caring
And one of their dedicated number
Searched all over a busy, packed church
On a Christmas Eve, but for my sister and I
Two seats together were found.

I remember the congregation being first to hear
A wonderful girls choir, not known before
Then sumptuous recordings were on sale
Thus a whole new dynasty was born.

These Abbey Maidens flew the nest
But many returned as Alumni, singing so well
How sweet to see them once again.

The school holidays bring their own delights
A treat we had in store,
The Royal School of Church Music

Provided Anthems with Introits galore.

Grown up choirs also visit when the girls,
The boys are taking a well earned break.

The wonderful choir of boys with men
Are robed in blue and white
The boys' attire includes a ruff
In the style of Good Queen Bess!

The maidens sport a robe of cream
With tabard all of Lincoln Green
The front has a cross in contrasting shade
Clearly seen as the procession is held.

We had a visit from the choir of Atlantic College
The amazing International sixth form school
Down at Llantwit Major, a memory for me
A lovely service and not forgetting
The concert with a Wing Commander
Who led a military band to raise a mint of funds.

What poem on Bath Abbey then
Would ever be complete
Without a tribute to the choirs, their Directors
Plus the organists making a great team,

A long line of training for songsters pray twice it's said!

A new tradition started here
The Rector made a call to bring
Our scores of Handel, that all may sing
Hallelujah to the King!

We made our best and joyous sounds,
The music reverberated all around
Our choir played it's goodly part
While the music is very dear to my heart.

See this image, hear us sing
Hope for every living thing
Trumpet stop on organ here
Raise the rafters, sing one's heart out
Like never before!

It was an ordinary Sunday, once upon a time
When we were asked to test the tannoy
Commenting on how we heard the sermon,
The prayers, the reading and of course the choir.

I chose a seat, 'twas quite far back, it's number WW1

But I was seated right beside a loudspeaker, and
I was able to report that everything during the whole service
Was clear, as I could hear it all without exception,
So this I reported on my sheet of yellow paper
Handing that in for Dean and Chapter.

The service was of Choral Mattins
Now replaced with Sung Eucharist
But back in the day I really noticed
How the sermon was nearly at the end
Unlike Communion when it's part way through!

One lovely, happy Sunday morning
A Baptism was held at our big, stone font
Many stood up and I crossed the floor
To wish Grandsire peace, now and evermore.

I have a friend of many years standing
Who doesn't like the shaking of hands
But I will turn 360 degrees
To greet all others, all around me!

The peace can take the unsuspecting
Almost completely by surprise

The touch was banned all during Covid
Then the people had to make a safe bow.

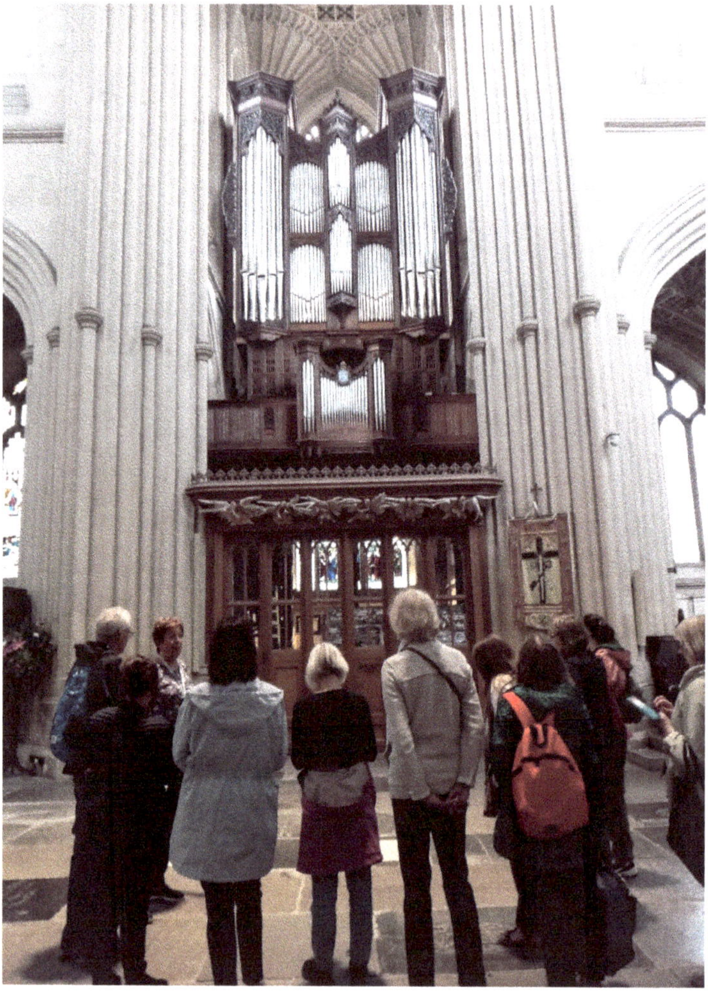

Part Four – Come Inside!

A warm welcome awaits each soul
Deep within this aged door
Opened wide, receive within
Blessings, bread and wine divine.

Innumerable generations have served this place
Shining, loving warmth of grace
Every service and every day
Meet and greet the Christian way.

The poem that lasts the whole of this book
Started with the bells,
Let's not forget how audible these are
Across the City far and wide
A call to worship, to come inside.

The joy of hearing bells ring out
Can transcend human words
But all the comfort that one needs
Is found at this the Altar
A solace when life falters.

While admiring the architecture
Take in the whole, see the candles

That a Lady Verger their secret told.
These at the choir stalls in fact
Are oil lamps of brass with white to look
Like candles, but if you get closer you will see
A wick inside an oil repository.

The Lady Verger would fill the oil
Then trim the wicks to perfect the whole.

Venture through the North West porch
Where all may pass to feast their eyes
Pause to view a glass panel in the floor
A Walk of Faith through which you see
A Norman Arch, a perfect bow, atop a pillar
These the remains of an ancient building,
A lower level than Bishop Oliver's existing church.

Norman arches went out of vogue
But in came a Perpendicular style
The broken arch for humanity's fall.

Remember Wells? Our sister church,
With its glorious scissor arch
Was the first of all English Cathedrals
To be built all completely Perpendicular.

Bath Abbey's North Transept
Has a winding, wooden stair
This is the way to the organ loft
Route to play the King of Instruments
Our new Mighty Klais found there.

Should you enter around half term
Many crafts for the young you'll learn
See the children gathered around
A block of Bath stone in a bowl
While little ones work their magic chisels
But such a dear, little girl, almost too small to see
Dawdled with Grandsire to whom I reached
My hand in prayer because both he
And His Honour loved to hear
About my colleague, whose fate I followed.

More latterly, the year was 2024
Bath Abbey opened wide it's Great West door,
Music for Palm Sunday filled the skies
As all around folk gathered there.

A Lady Vicar robed in red
Was speaking very earnestly

To just a few Parishioners
For whom the Reverend was all ears.

I took my turn to be remembered
As we spoke just briefly then,
She asked me would I write a book
So This Firm Foundation thus was born.

I hope the pages entertained,
That you like the pictures too
If you've enjoyed it's pages here
Then come inside and learn still more.

At a time that I remember
Easter started at first light
With the burning of a fire
In the doorway of our West Front.

The Lady Vicar lit for Easter
Reviving ancient Holy rite.
This was followed by a breakfast
Hot, delicious coffee served.

Then a gentle, man departed
For a church complete with retreat
So we gave him a farewell supper

At Abbey Church House, sadly now sold.

You could say those were golden years
But still the church lives on,
Pre Covid numbers are now returning
After all the social distancing is finally gone.

We can now attend without a mask
The church is open, no need to ask
And if you happen to reside
With your proof from the Council
Then it's free, with guides to talk of all that special history.

Find a comfort, a space to pray
A Chaplain to talk to, on a weekday
Learn of all the work of folk
Who keep the church running
Everyday and every way.

An informal service at six-thirty
Welcomes Abbey's under thirties
While mature generations often speak
For one, on healing, was heard to preach.

A doctor by trade as well as a priest

The story was of the miracles of Christ
And also how Recovery could still occur
He cradled a baby that had grown to a child
After prayers were said at the hospital bedside.

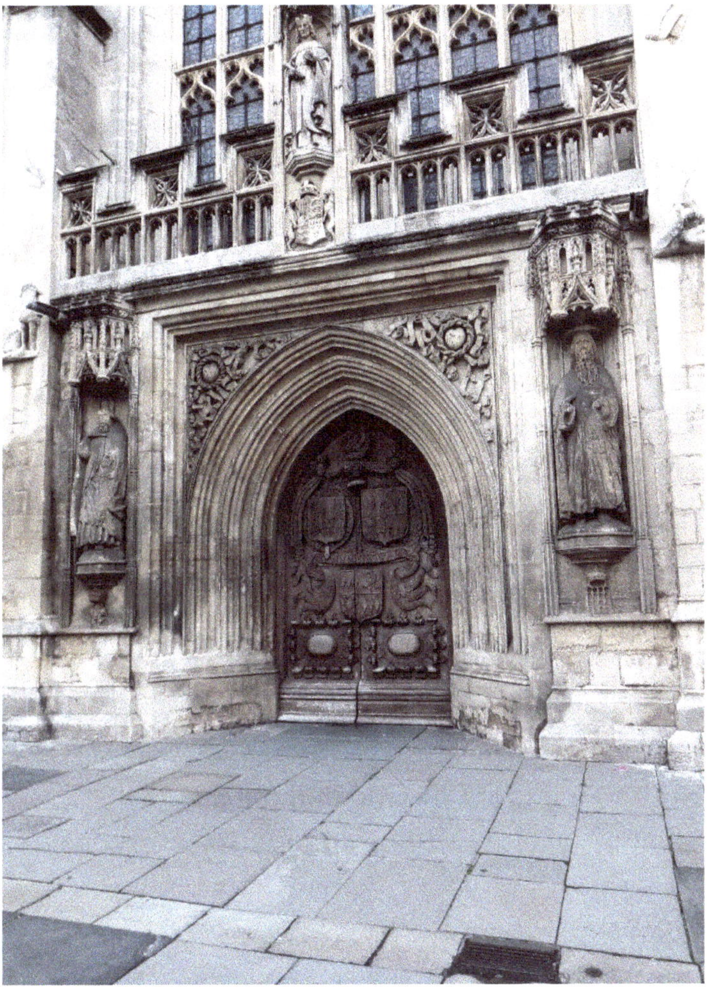

Loving kindness everywhere
Bags of food at Harvest there
Pentecost, a big appeal
Mission five did really well!

We met our wonderful Zambian partners
We heard from a couple speaking online
Of amazing work in Jerusalem and Palestine.

Truly this a Global Church
Growing, thriving, still in touch
Surviving Covid with sublime
Thoughts every day so well expressed
Available to the whole world online.

Reaching out, Oh! Fairest building
In our World Heritage City
Carved in local stone of honey.

Built to the glory of God and King,
Shelter, sanctuary, hope and joy for everyone.

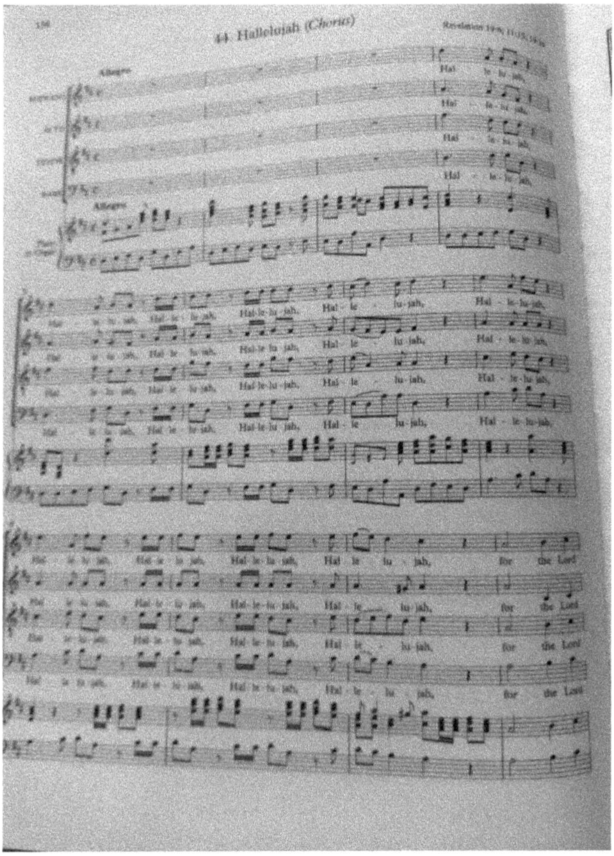
44. Hallelujah (Chorus)
Allegro
Hal - le - lu - jah,
for the Lord

Index of Colour Images

Author Profile.	Page 1
Bath Abbey Bells.	Page 6
Bath Abbey Exterior, Southside.	22
Carillon Close up.	6
Carved Angel, choir stalls.	24
Chapel of Gethsemane.	30
Crossing and Lectern.	32
East End Exterior.	36
Great West Door.	68
High Altar with Trinity Frontal.	39
Interior Lichfield Cathedral.	41
Interior Wells Cathedral.	54
Mighty Klais Organ.	61
Music Score, Handel.	70
Nave and Crossing roof.	28
Ringing Chamber.	11
Southside, Lichfield Cathedral.	44
South Transept, Bath Abbey.	50
St. Alphege Chapel.	48
Statue of the Risen Lord.	52
Tenor Bell.	9
The Mineral Water Hospital.	17
Tower Top Pinnacle.	27
View from Camden Crescent.	35

View from the Abbey Tower
        (i)   Looking west.   15
        (ii)   Looking north   15
West Front, Lichfield Cathedral.   43

References

Bath Abbey's Monuments – An Illustrated History.   Oliver Taylor
The History Press 2023

G.F. Handel. Messiah, Vocal Score. Edited by Clifford Bartlett. Music Department, Oxford University Press 1998.

The People who made Wells Cathedral more than Stone and Glass. Simon Garrett and Anne Crawford, Photography Philip Nash 2013 Heritage Films and Publications Ltd.